Saturn

Saturn

Elaine Landau

Watts LIBRARY

Franklin Watts
A Division of Grolier Publishing
New York • London • Hong Kong • Sydney
Danbury, Connecticut

For Michael—our future astronaut

Note to readers: Definitions for words in **bold** can be found in the Glossary at the back of this book.

Photographs ©: Astron Society of the Pacific: 36, 43; Bridgeman Art Library International Ltd., London/New York: 8 (Private Collection), Corbis-Bettmann: 12; Finley Holiday Film: 21, 38, 42; NASA: 51 (ESA), 44, 47 (JPL), 2, 23, 24, 31, 37, 39 top, 40, 41; Photo Researchers: 5 top, 15 (Science Photo Library), 34 (Space Telescope Science Institute/NASA/SPL), 6 (NASA/Science Source), 7 bottom, 48 (European Space Agency/SPL), 29 (Ludek Pesek/SPL), 30 (Chris Buttler/SPL), 46 (David Ducros/SPL); Photri: 17, 26, 32, 39 bottom; Superstock, Inc.: 9; Tom Stack & Associates: cover (NASA/JPL/Tsado), 18 (ESA/Tsado).

Solar system diagram created by Greg Harris

Visit Franklin Watts on the Internet at:
http://publishing.grolier.com

Library of Congress Cataloging-in-Publication Data

Landau, Elaine.
    Saturn / Elaine Landau.
        p.   cm.— (Watts Library)
    Includes bibliographical references and index.
    Summary: Discusses what we know about the size, density, atmosphere, rings, and moons of Saturn, as well as what we may learn in the future.
    ISBN: 0-531-20389-1 (lib. bdg.)   0-531-16430-6 (pbk.)
    1. Saturn (Planet)—Juvenile literature. [1. Saturn (Planet)] I. Title. II. Series.
QB671.L36 1999
523.46—dc21

98-465268
CIP
AC

Contents

This view of Saturn shows the planet's true golden color.

Chapter One

The Ringed Planet

Saturn is a large and beautiful planet. When ancient stargazers looked into the night sky thousands of years ago, they saw Saturn as a bright golden object. The ancient Romans named the planet after their god of planting and harvest. The god Saturn was married to Ops, the goddess of plenty.

Saturn is one of the nine planets that make up our **solar system**. The solar system consists of the Sun and the nine planets, dozens of moons, **comets**, and

The Roots of Christmas

Every year, the ancient Romans honored the god Saturn with a week-long feast known as the Saturnalia. During the celebration, prisoners were freed from jail as an act of goodwill, Roman armies were not permitted to start any new wars, and schools and shops remained closed so that everyone could enjoy the festivities. Some historians think that a number of our modern Christmas customs, such as having large dinners with family and friends and exchanging gifts, can be traced back to the Saturnalia.

asteroids that **orbit**, or move around, the Sun. As you can see in the illustration on pages 10 and 11, Saturn is the sixth planet from the Sun. It is the farthest planet that can be seen from Earth with the naked eye.

The planet Saturn was first viewed through a telescope by an Italian **astronomer** named Galileo Galilei in 1610. When

Galileo looked at Saturn, he was surprised by what he saw. He expected Saturn to be round, but the planet seemed to have puffy bulges on both sides. In his description of the planet, Galileo wrote that Saturn had "ears."

This painting shows Galileo explaining how to use a telescope.

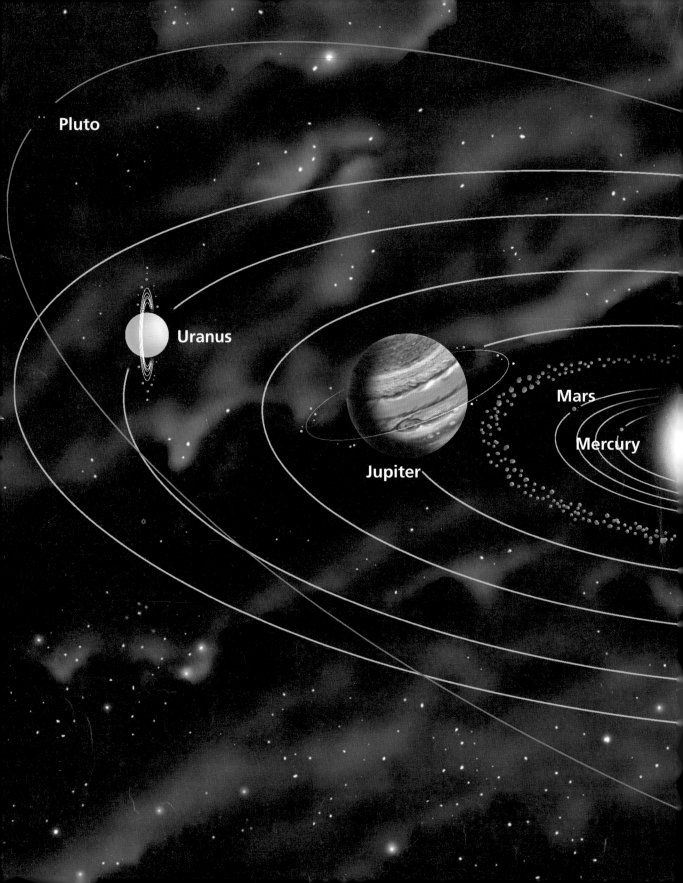

The Solar System

Venus

Moon

Earth

Asteroid Belt

Saturn

Neptune

Dutch astronomer Christiaan Huygens was the first person to suggest that Saturn had a ring around it.

Giovanni Domenico Cassini (1625–1712) spent a good deal of time studying Saturn.

In 1656, a Dutch astronomer named Christiaan Huygens also noted the bulges on both sides of Saturn. Because Huygens had a more powerful telescope than Galileo's, he was able to see Saturn's "ears" more clearly. He suggested that the planet was surrounded by a ring. This was a startling idea. As far as scientists knew, no other planet in the solar system had a ring around it.

In 1675, a French-Italian astronomer named Giovanni Domenico Cassini spent quite a bit of time studying Saturn. He noticed a dark band within the ring and realized that the band was probably a gap between two separate rings. To honor the scientist for his incredible discovery, the gap was named Cassini's Division. Today we know that Saturn is surrounded by many rings.

Saturn on the Move

Like Earth and all the other planets in the solar system, Saturn orbits the Sun. Earth orbits the Sun in 365 days, or 1 year. Because a year is defined as the amount of time it takes for a planet to revolve around the Sun once, the farther a planet is from the Sun, the longer its year is. Saturn is about nine and a half times farther from the Sun than Earth, so 1 year on Saturn lasts about 29 1/2 Earth-years!

Saturn—and all the objects in our solar system—revolve around the Sun because they are trapped by a powerful, but invisible force called **gravity**. The Sun's gravity pulls all the planets and other objects in the solar system toward the Sun. In the same way, Earth's gravity pulls the Moon and objects on our planet toward the center of Earth.

The force of gravity operates all around us. For example, if a circus juggler doesn't catch the objects he or she tosses into the air, they will fall to the ground. Gravity is the force that pulls them down. The same gravitational force causes leaves to drop in autumn and snowflakes to fall in winter.

Earth is not the only planet affected by gravity. The same gravitational pull we experience on Earth occurs on Saturn and the other planets in the solar system. Saturn's gravitational pull is slightly stronger than Earth's.

The Changing Seasons

Like Earth, Saturn experiences weather changes and seasons. Because a year on Saturn is much longer than a year on Earth, each season on Saturn is longer too. Believe it or not, each of Saturn's seasons is about 7 1/2 years long.

A Pudgy Planet

Because Saturn rotates so fast, the materials that make up the planet are spun outward along its **equator**. As a result, the planet bulges at its center and flattens at its poles.

As Saturn orbits the Sun, it also **rotates**, or turns, on its **axis**—an imaginary line through the center of a planet. All planets rotate on an axis like a toy top. Earth rotates once every 23 hours and 56 minutes. Even though Saturn is much larger than Earth, it spins much faster. Saturn rotates once every 10 hours and 39 minutes. That means a day on Saturn is much shorter than a day on Earth.

Saturn's Magnetic Field

Besides a gravitational field, many planets have a **magnetic field**. A planet's magnetic field is similar to the magnetic field around the magnets built into the door of your refrigerator. Have you ever noticed that it is hard to open a refrigerator door just a little? The attraction between the magnets inside the door and the magnets along the door frame pull the door closed. If you open the door a little more, you do not feel the same pull because the magnets are no longer influenced by one another's magnetic fields.

Saturn's gravity keeps its moons orbiting the planet. This view of Saturn and some of its moons was created with a computer. Color-enhanced images of Saturn, Mimas, Enceladus, Tethys, Dione, Rhea, and Titan were combined with artwork of Hyperion's surface. The image does not show the planets to scale or in the proper positions along their orbital paths.

The Queen of the Planets

Jupiter is often called the king of the planets because it is the largest planet and because it is named after king of the Roman gods. Saturn is often called the queen of the planets because it is the second largest planet and because it is so beautiful.

The magnetic field of a planet is much larger than the magnetic field of the magnets in your refrigerator. Saturn's magnetic field stretches for millions of miles. Earth has a magnetic field, too, but it is much weaker than Saturn's.

How Saturn Measures Up

Saturn is the second largest planet in the solar system. Only Jupiter is larger. Saturn is approximately 74,900 miles (120,500 km) across. That makes it nearly ten times wider than Earth.

Because Saturn is so large, it also has a lot of **mass**. In other words, it contains a lot of material. Saturn's mass is ninety-five times greater than Earth's. Jupiter is the only planet in the solar system with a greater mass than Saturn.

Mass is not the only measurement that scientists use to compare planets. They also look at **density**. Density describes the relationship between mass—the total amount of material in an object—and **volume**—the total amount of space the object occupies. To find an object's density, you can divide its mass by its volume.

Imagine one measuring cup full of popped popcorn and a second measuring cup full of uncooked popcorn kernels. Which is denser? Think about it. Popped popcorn is light and fluffy. Corn kernels are smaller and heavier. When the volume of corn kernels and popcorn is equal, the mass of the corn kernels is much greater. This means that the density of the corn kernels is also much greater.

The planet Saturn has more mass than most other planets, so you might expect it to be one of the densest. But don't forget, Saturn is also much larger than most other planets. In other words, it has a much greater volume than those planets. Actually, Saturn is the least dense planet in the solar system. Earth—the densest planet in the solar system—is about eight times denser than Saturn.

Jupiter is the only planet larger than Saturn.

In this view of Earth from space, you can clea... see South America and parts of No... America and Africa. The b... areas are ocean, and... white areas are... clouds in Eart... atmosphe...

Chapter Two

A Gas Giant

Have you ever seen a photograph of Earth taken from space? The first thing you notice are the white swirling clouds in our **atmosphere**. Below the clouds, you can see bright blue oceans and greenish-brown land.

When you look at an image of Saturn taken by a spacecraft, you can see the colorful bands of clouds that make up its atmosphere, but you don't see any solid surface below them. That's because Saturn is not a solid planet the way Earth is. It a gas giant—a huge ball of gases and liquids. Jupiter, Neptune, and Uranus are gas giants, too.

Saturn's Atmosphere

While Earth's atmosphere consists mostly of nitrogen and oxygen, the most common gases in Saturn's atmosphere are hydrogen and helium. Saturn's atmosphere is much deeper than Earth's. In other words, it extends many more miles into the planet's interior.

The clouds in Saturn's atmosphere have beautiful bands of pale gold, beige, and white. The clouds on Earth are made of water vapor, but the clouds on Saturn are made mostly of ammonia and methane. On Earth, these gases are invisible, but because the queen of the planets is so much farther from the Sun, it is much colder. At the outer edge of the Saturn's clouds, the temperature may drop as low as –285 degrees Fahrenheit (–176 degrees Celsius). As a result, the gases in its atmosphere are frozen. The lovely bands you see when you look at Saturn are actually made of solid ice crystals.

Like the clouds on Earth, Saturn's clouds are always moving. This move-

This color-enhanced view clearly shows the bands of clouds in Saturn's atmosphere. These bands are made of solid ice crystals.

Winds of a World

Most of Saturn's winds blow in an easterly direction. They may reach speeds of more than 1,100 miles (1,770 kilometers) per hour. That's more than three times faster than the winds of a tornado—the strongest winds on Earth.

ment causes powerful gusting winds and raging storms. Some of these storms are so large that they can be seen from space.

Inside Saturn

What lies beneath Saturn's colorful clouds? Scientists think that Saturn's massive atmosphere puts a great deal of pressure on the materials deep within the planet. Because the pressure inside Saturn is so much greater than the pressure on Earth, some scientists believe the hydrogen far below Saturn's atmosphere exists as a liquid. This liquid metallic hydrogen layer forms Saturn's surface. At the very center of Saturn is a rocky **core**. Scientists think Saturn's core is about the same size as the entire Earth.

The interior of Saturn is also much warmer than the atmosphere. Scientists aren't sure exactly where the heat comes from. Some researchers think it is created as helium slowly sinks through the liquid metallic hydrogen deep within the planet. Others believe that Saturn has an internal energy source that was created when the planet formed.

According to this theory, a great deal of energy was released when the materials that make up the planet Saturn came together billions of years ago. The energy was trapped deep inside the planet and is now slowly escaping as heat moves toward the planet's surface. This idea explains an important difference between Earth and Saturn. While Earth gets most of its heat and light energy from the Sun, Saturn gives off about twice as much energy as it receives from the Sun.

Scientists have never seen what lies below Saturn's clouds, but they have theories about what the planet's interior is made of.

A group of engineers and technicians at the Kennedy Space Center in Cape Canaveral, Florida prepares Pioneer 11 for its 1973 launch.

Chapter Three

Saturn's Rings

In 1973, the United States launched an unmanned spacecraft to study Jupiter and Saturn. The spacecraft, named *Pioneer 11*, flew within 13,000 miles (20,900 km) of Saturn in September 1979 and sent back photographs of the mysterious planet. Information collected by *Pioneer 11* allowed scientists to discover two new rings around the planet.

In 1977, the United States launched two more **space probes** to study Saturn as well as Jupiter, Neptune, and Uranus.

In November 1980, the first probe—*Voyager 1*—flew within 78,000 miles (126,000 km) of the queen of the planets. It sent back images of something scientists had never seen before—spokes on Saturn's rings. These light and dark objects look similar to the spokes on a bicycle wheel as they rotate around Saturn along with the rings. Scientists think the spokes may be dust particles.

In August 1981, the second probe—*Voyager 2*—flew even closer to the queen of the planets. It was just 63,000 miles (101,000 km) from Saturn. Both Voyager spacecraft provided scientists with new information about the planet, and images of Saturn, its moons, and its most famous features of all—its rings.

As you learned in Chapter 1, in 1656, Christiaan Huygens realized that Saturn was surrounded by at least one ring. As more powerful telescopes were invented, scientists realized that there was more than one ring circling Saturn's equator. Some thought there were three or four; others thought there might be as many as six rings.

Today we know that Saturn's ring system consists of several major rings. Each of these major rings is actually made up of many closely spaced, slender ringlets. There may be as many as 10,000 ringlets in all. Even though scientists have learned a

A computer created this color-enhanced view of Saturn's rings by combining many images taken by Voyager 2. You can see that the planet's major rings are made up of many closely spaced slender rings.

Saturn's Ring System

Name of Feature	Width	Description
D-Ring	7,800 miles (12,600 km)	Saturn's innermost ring; it is very faint
Guerin Division	750 miles (1,200 km)	The narrow gap between the D-Ring and the C-Ring
C-Ring	11,000 miles (18,000 km)	The third ring to be discovered; one of the three main rings that can be seen from Earth; the A-Ring and the B-Ring are the other main rings
Maxwell the Division	300 miles (500 km)	The very narrow gap between the C-Ring and the B-Ring
B-Ring	14,600 miles (23,500 km)	The second ring to be discovered; one of the three main rings that can be seen from Earth; the A-Ring and the C-Ring are the other main rings
Cassini Division	3,000 miles (4,800 km)	The first gap to be discovered; it separates the A-Ring and the B-Ring; it can be seen from Earth
Huygens Gap	150 to 250 miles (250 to 400 km)	A small region within the Cassini Division
A-Ring	9,700 miles (15,600 km)	The first ring to be discovered; one of the three main rings that can be seen from Earth; the B-Ring and the C-Ring are the other main rings
Encke Division	3,400 miles (5,460 km)	A faint gap in the outer portion of the A-Ring
F-Ring	Unknown	A very narrow, but fairly bright ring
G-Ring	Unknown	A very faint ring
E-Ring	14,900 miles (24,000 km)	The ring farthest from Saturn; it is very faint

great deal about Saturn's ring system in the last few decades, there are still many questions left to answer.

Scientists know what the rings are made of—trillions of pieces of ice. Some of these pieces are as small as a grain of sand; others are as large as a barn. The rings may also contain dust and rock. If you could measure Saturn's ring system from one edge to the other, you'd find out that they are more than 600,000 miles (1,000,000 km) wide. That's about two and a half times the distance from Earth to the Moon. Amazingly, the rings are no more than 1 mile (1.6 km) thick.

Scientists believe that Saturn's rings are made of millions of pieces of ice. This illustration shows what Saturn's rings might look like close up.

Shepherd Moons

The Voyager spacecraft discovered that some of the particles in Saturn's rings may be held in place by three tiny shepherd moons. Scientists believe that a shepherd moon helps to keep the particles in Saturn's rings together the way a shepherd keeps his or her animals in a herd. You will learn more about the shepherd moons —Atlas, Prometheus, and Pandora—in Chapter 4.

Rings Around the Planet

Just as Saturn orbits the Sun, Saturn's rings orbit the planet. In fact, each of the particles that makes up the rings has its own orbit. Separately, each particle moves around Saturn as if it were a moon. Together, they form the incredible rings that circle the planet.

Where Do Rings Come From?

No one knows how old Saturn's rings are. Some scientists think that the rings formed at the same time as Saturn. Others believe they may have formed much later—when some of Saturn's moons crashed into one another or were split into pieces by a comet or an asteroid.

It is also possible that new rings are in the process of forming right now. In 1995, a number of unidentified clumps of material were spotted close to the edge of Saturn's rings. Were these clumps once moons? Scientists will watch them closely to see if they start to spread out and form new rings.

Sometimes the pieces of ice that make up Saturn's rings stray from their orbit and crash into one another. In some cases, the dust on the surface of the particles is hurled into space. In other cases, the particles break into smaller pieces. Some of these smaller pieces may rejoin to form new particles. Whenever two pieces collide, their orbits change, so each may end up hitting other particles.

This view of Saturn and six of its moons is a collage of color-enhanced Voyager images. It was created by NASA scientists using a computer. The moons are not shown to scale, but they are in their proper positions relative to the planet. How many moons can you find in this view?

Chapter Four

The Moons of Saturn

Saturn has more moons than any other planet in our solar system. It has eighteen named moons, and as many as twelve others have been sighted in recent years. These moons have not been named because scientists do not yet know enough about them and their orbital paths to be sure that they are all separate moons.

The first thirteen moons were discovered by scientists using telescopes. Many of these moons were spotted at a specific

This color-enhanced view of Saturn shows its rings on edge in relation to our planet. Because the rings almost disappear at this angle, the planet's moons are more visible to viewers on Earth.

point in Saturn's orbit. Every 15 years or so, Saturn's rings are turned on edge in relation to Earth. As a result, the rings nearly disappear from view. At these times, the brightly glowing rings do not dominate our view of Saturn, so scientists are able to get a better glimpse of the planet's moons.

Most of Saturn's moons are made of ice and rock and have many **craters** on their surfaces. These craters were made when objects in space, such as asteroids or comets, crashed into the moons. Most of Saturn's moons are round, but a few

Two New Moons?

During a 10-hour period in 1995, the Hubble Space Telescope—a giant telescope that orbits Earth—took twenty-seven photographs of what appears to be two previously unknown moons. For now, scientists are calling these moons S/1995 S3 and S/1995 S4, but they may soon be named. If they are, Saturn will have twenty named moons.

Saturn's Named Moons

Name	Distance from Saturn		Distance Across		Year of Discovery
Pan	83,000 miles	(133,000 km)	12 miles	(19 km)	1990
Atlas	85,000 miles	(137,000 km)	19 miles	(30 km)	1980
Prometheus	86,000 miles	(139,000 km)	135 miles	(220 km)	1980
Pandora	88,000 miles	(142,000 km)	125 miles	(200 km)	1980
Epimetheus	94,000 miles	(151,000 km)	55 miles	(90 km)	1980
Janus	94,000 miles	(151,000 km)	60 miles	(100 km)	1980
Mimas	117,000 miles	(188,000 km)	240 miles	(390 km)	1789
Enceladus	149,000 miles	(240,000 km)	310 miles	(500 km)	1789
Calypso	185,000 miles	(298,000 km)	22 miles	(35 km)	1980
Telesto	185,000 miles	(298,000 km)	22 miles	(35 km)	1980
Tethys	185,000 miles	(298,000 km)	650 miles	(1050 km)	1684
Dione	235,000 miles	(379,000 km)	700 miles	(1120 km)	1684
Helene	235,000 miles	(379,000 km)	100 miles	(160 km)	1980
Rhea	328,000 miles	(528,000 km)	950 miles	(1530 km)	1672
Titan	759,000 miles	(1,221,000 km)	3,190 miles	(5140 km)	1655
Hyperion	993,000 miles	(1,502,000 km)	220 miles	(360 km)	1848
Iapetus	2,211,000 miles	(3,559,000 km)	890 miles	(1440 km)	1617
Phoebe	6,576,000 miles	(10,583,000 km)	125 miles	(200 km)	1898

have unusual shapes. Some of the smaller, recently discovered moons are egg-shaped with bumpy **terrain**. Scientists suspect that these moons may have broken off from larger moons when they were struck by comets or asteroids.

A Closer Look at some Moons

The distance across Mimas is about the same as the distance from Sioux Falls, South Dakota, to Des Moines, Iowa. This little moon has a huge crater named Herschel. Herschel is so large that it occupies about one-third of the moon's **diameter**. This crater was probably formed when a large object whirling

A number of images were combined and color enhanced to produce this detailed view of Mimas. Notice the small moon's large crater.

A number of images from Voyager 2 *were combined to create this view of Enceladus. The colors of the moon were enhanced by photographing it through violet and green filters.*

through space collided with Mimas. If the impact had been any greater, Mimas might have broken apart.

Unlike Mimas, Enceladus has no large craters. It does have some small ones, but some regions have no craters at all. In some areas, the smooth surface of the moon is marked with long grooves. The surface of Enceladus reflects almost 100 percent of the sunlight that strikes it, so it looks like a glowing ball.

The surface of Tethys consists mostly of frozen water. Like Mimas, Tethys has one very large crater. This crater—named Odysseus—takes up about one-third of Tethys's diameter and is nearly 250 miles (400 km) deep. Tethys also has a wide canyon named Ithaca Chasma that stretches most of the way around the moon.

Dione and Tethys are considered sister moons. Dione is a little larger, but quite a bit denser that Tethys. As a result, scientists believe that Dione contains more solid material, such as

rock, than Tethys. Much of Dione is covered with craters, but it also has valleys and smooth areas. Scientists believe the moon's large light-colored areas are covered with ice.

Like Dione, Rhea is made up of rocky material and ice. However, Rhea appears to have more craters than any of Saturn's other moons. Scientists believe that it has been struck by many objects in the past. Parts of Rhea's surface are covered with large patches of frost.

Many of Dione's craters can be seen in this color-enhanced view created from several images taken by Voyager 1 *in 1980.*

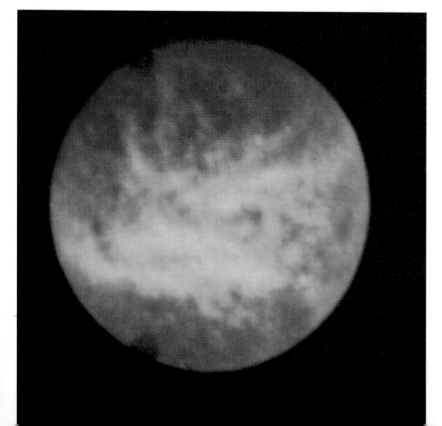

To create this color-enhanced view of Rhea, scientists combined three Voyager 1 *images. One image was taken through a violet filter; one image was taken through a blue filter; and one image was taken through an orange filter.*

Titan is Saturn's largest moon, and the second largest moon in the solar system. Only Jupiter's moon Ganymede is bigger. Titan is larger than the planets Mercury and Pluto.

Although Titan is a moon because it orbits a planet, some of its features make it more like a planet than like other moons. For example, it is the only moon in the solar system that has an atmosphere. This atmosphere is mostly nitrogen, just like Earth's atmosphere. Researchers suspect that Titan's atmosphere may be very similar to the atmosphere on Earth millions, or even billions, of years ago. If they are right, and there is liquid water on the moon, it is possible that early life forms might be developing on Titan right now.

This color-enhanced view of Titan gives us a good idea of what the moon actually looks like from space. Unlike most moons, Titan has a thick atmosphere. The clouds in the moon's upper atmosphere are orange.

Scientists aren't getting their hopes up though. It's very unlikely that liquid water exists on Titan. Because it is so far from the Sun, Titan is a very cold place. Temperatures as low as –290°F (–180°C) are not unusual.

For many years, scientists didn't know much about Titan because a deep layer of clouds in its upper atmosphere forms an orange-brown haze around it. Scientists say that Titan's haze is similar to the smog in Los Angeles, California, or

The Hubble Space Telescope

The gases in Earth's thick atmosphere distort what we see when we look into space. They make stars seem to twinkle and planets look fuzzy. For hundreds of years, stargazers built observatories on high mountains where the air is thinner and the view is clearer, but they always dreamed of having a telescope above Earth's atmosphere. Today, the Hubble Space Telescope, which is about the size of a school bus, orbits Earth and provides us with incredible views of objects inside—and outside—our solar system.

Tokyo, Japan. In fact, Titan is the smoggiest sphere in the solar system.

With the aid of the Hubble Space Telescope, Peter H. Smith and his colleagues at the University of Arizona became the first scientists to see beyond Titan's smog. The team of researchers took fifty pictures of Titan as the moon completed its 16-day orbit around Saturn. The images showed that Titan has at least one bright area about as big as Australia. The moon also has several large dark patches on its surface. Smith's team suggests that the bright area could be a mountain of frozen water and ammonia ice. The dark patches may be lakes or small oceans of ethane or methane. The researchers used the images to create a detailed map of Titan's surface.

Unlike most of Saturn's moons, Hyperion is irregularly shaped. It looks something like an overgrown squash. Some scientists think that Hyperion may be a piece of what was once a larger moon. That moon probably broke apart when it was

Most of Saturn's moons have round edges, but Hyperion is irregularly shaped.

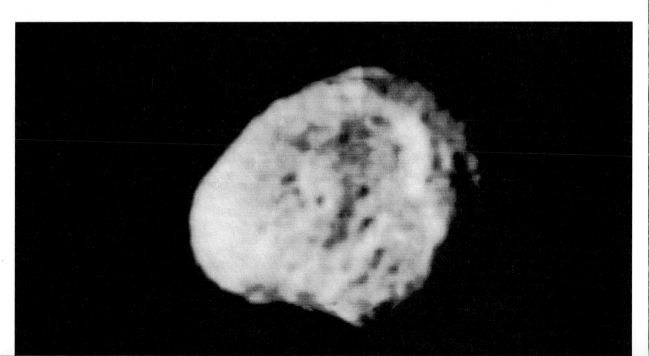

hit by another object. This would explain Hyperion's unusual shape.

Iapetus is also an unusual moon. One portion of Iapetus is white, shiny, and bright, while the other half is a dark rusty-red color. The border between the two regions is uneven and curved. Some scientists believe that the bright portion of Iapetus is made of ice, and the darker area is made of rock.

The bright, shining portion of Iapetus is clearly visible in this color-enhanced view of the moon. Scientists used a computer to combine several images into this single view.

Phoebe is a small moon with a very dark surface. Because Phoebe is so far from Saturn, it takes 550 Earth-days to complete one orbit around the queen of the planets. And while all the other moons orbit Saturn from east to west, Phoebe moves in the opposite direction.

Because Phoebe is so far from Saturn and has an unusual orbit, some scientists think that it hasn't always been one of Saturn's moons. It may have been an asteroid that became trapped by the mighty planet's gravity and began orbiting Saturn.

A giant Titan rocket with Cassini/Huygens on top blasted off from Kennedy Space Center in Cape Canaveral, Florida on October 15, 1997.

Chapter Five

The Cassini/ Huygens Mission

For centuries, skygazers and scientists have had very few answers to their questions about Saturn, its moons, and its rings. This may soon change. On October 15, 1997, the U.S. National Aeronautics and Space Administration (NASA) launched a space probe called *Cassini/Huygens* from Kennedy Space Center on Cape Canaveral in Florida.

Why does the trip to Saturn take so long? You might think that it takes this long because Saturn is so far away. Even though Saturn is more than 760 million miles (1.3 billion km) away, a trip directly from Earth to Saturn would not take 7 years.

Cassini/Huygens was not launched on a direct path to Saturn. In fact, it was sent toward Venus, not Saturn. In order to reach Saturn, the spacecraft needs to pick up speed along the way. *Cassini/Huygens* will get the boost it needs from the gravity of other planets. Before the spacecraft reaches Saturn, it will pass Venus twice, come back around Earth, and then go on toward Jupiter. As the spacecraft passes each of these planets, it will use the pull from their gravitational fields to increase its speed.

When *Cassini/Huygens* finally reaches Saturn, an onboard rocket engine will fire and act like a brake to slow the spacecraft down. Then *Cassini/Huygens* will begin to circle the

This illustration shows what Cassini/Huygens *might look like as it travels through space.*

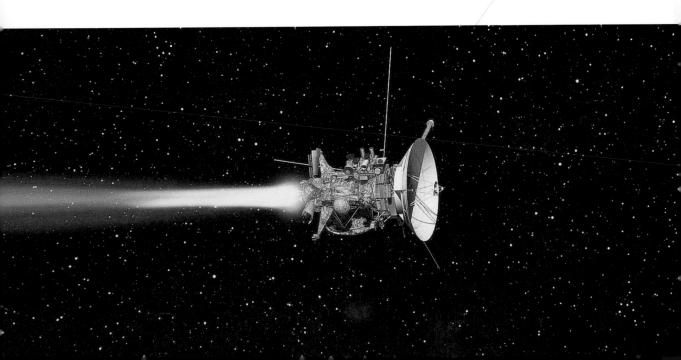

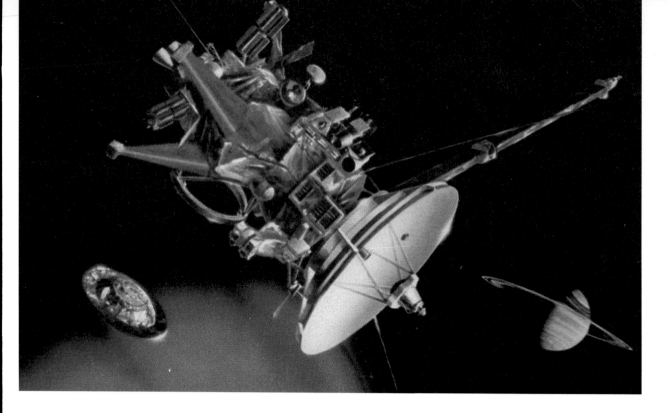

planet. During the *Cassini Saturn Orbiter*'s 4-year mission, it will circle the planet a total of seventy times. In November 2004, the *Huygens Titan Probe* will separate from the main spacecraft and drop into Titan's thick atmosphere. The probe has three parachutes and a heatshield to protect its aluminum body from heat caused by **friction**.

Researchers don't know whether the probe will land on a solid or liquid surface. We will not know exactly what the moon's surface is like until we see images taken by the probe. If everything goes according to plan, the *Huygens Probe* will take more than 1,100 photographs of Titan's surface and transmit them to the *Cassini Orbiter*. The orbiter will then send the images to NASA scientists on Earth.

An artist's representation of the Huygens Titan Probe separating from the Cassini Saturn Orbiter

This illustrations shows the Huygens Probe *on the surface of Titan.*

What the Names Mean

The *Huygens Titan Probe* was named for Dutch astronomer Christiaan Huygens. Huygens discovered Titan and identified Saturn's ring system. The *Cassini Saturn Orbiter* was named after Giovanni Domenico Cassini, the French-Italian astronomer who identified the gap between Saturn's A-Ring and B-Ring.

Besides showing us exactly what's beneath the giant moon's orangish-brown haze, the *Huygens Probe* will collect and analyze samples of the chemicals in Titan's atmosphere. A microphone on board the probe will detect any noises coming from the moon's surface. These might include the sound of wind blowing, rocks cracking, or ice crunching. It may also detect claps of thunder.

Goals of the Cassini/Huygens Mission

Titan	The *Huygens Probe* will study the moon's surface. The *Cassini Orbiter* will use radar to take additional images of the surface. Other instruments will measure the moon's temperature and the effect of Saturn's magnetic field on Titan.
Enceladus	The spacecraft will determine whether this moon has an internal source of heat and look for evidence of volcanoes on the surface. Materials from erupting volcanoes might float into space and feed the planet's rings.
Iapetus	Scientists hope to learn more about the dark portion of this moon. They would like to know whether the dark material comes from the moon itself or whether it came from some outside source.
Other Moons	The *Cassini Orbiter* will pass close to a number of other moons. Special cameras onboard will be able to take detailed photographs of their surfaces. These cameras are so sensitive that they could detect objects and features about the size of a barn.
Saturn's Rings	Are the rings made up of pieces of moons shattered by Saturn's gravitational pull or by comets and asteroids? Researcher's hope *Cassini/Huygens* will shed new light on this question.
Saturn's Magnetism	Saturn's **magnetosphere**—the area of space surrounding the planet that is affected by its magnetic field—may hold clues to other important occurrences on this giant planet. The Cassini/Huygens mission will attempt to learn more about how trapped particles within the planet's magnetosphere behave. It will also study the effect of Saturn's magnetic field on the planet's moons and rings.
Saturn's Atmosphere	The orbiter will collect information about the forces that cause Saturn's raging winds and storms. If all goes well, it will also photograph various levels of the planet's atmosphere.

Building Cassini/Huygens

Cassini/Huygens is the most complex spacecraft ever sent into space. Building and operating it requires the skills of scientists all over the world. NASA's Jet Propulsion Laboratory in Pasadena, California, designed and built the orbiter. Data from the orbiter will be relayed through the agency's Deep Space Network stations in California, Spain, and Australia. The *Huygens Probe* was built by the European Space Agency—a group of space scientists funded by several Western European nations. The spacecraft's radio, antenna, and some of its scientific instruments came from the Italian Space Agency.

To help ensure the spacecraft's success, scientists tried to develop equipment that cannot break. For example, the data recorders have no moving parts, so they can't jam. The equipment was also designed so that no single failure could end the mission. Even the back-up systems have their own back-up systems.

Opposite: A technician prepares the Huygens Probe *for its long journey to Titan*

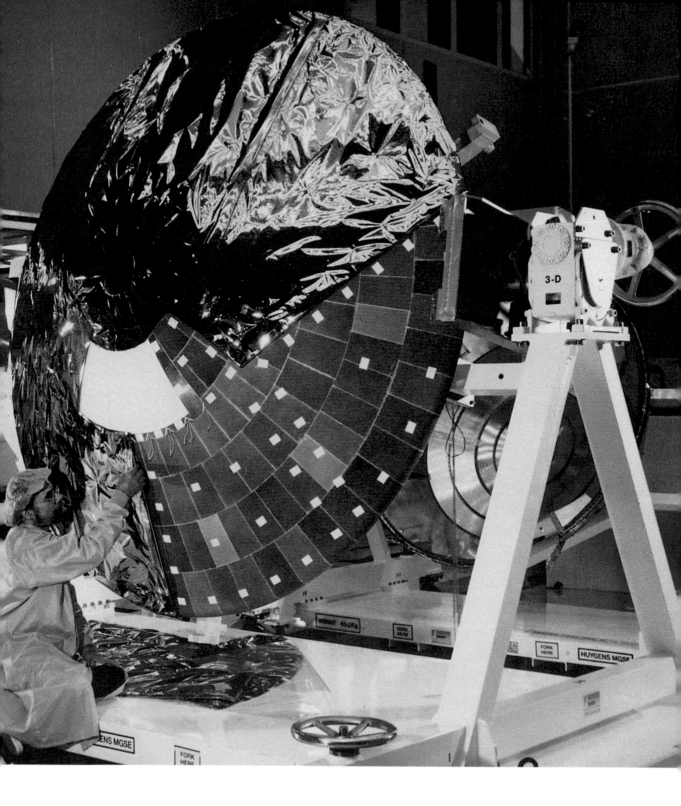

51

Even before *Cassini/Huygens* was launched, it had already proved beneficial in a number of ways. The technology created to explore Saturn was soon modified for smaller space missions. This resulted in substantial cost savings for the United States. Also, some of the equipment developed for the mission has been adapted for use by the military and communication companies.

Scientists hope that *Cassini/Huygens* will be beneficial in other ways when it reaches the queen of the planets. People first learned that Saturn was special in 1610 when Galileo looked through his telescope and saw "ears." Since then, more powerful telescopes and space probes have provided us with additional information about this beautiful golden planet. Scientists can hardly wait to see what secrets the Cassini/ Huygens mission will reveal.

Glossary

asteroid—a large piece of rock that formed at the same time as the Sun and planets.

astronomer—a scientist who studies objects in space. Today the term "space scientist" is more commonly used.

atmosphere—the various gases that surround a planet or other body in space.

axis—the imaginary line running from pole to pole through a planet's center. The planet spins, or rotates, along its axis.

comet—a small ball of rock and ice that orbits the Sun. When it gets close to the Sun, some of the ice melts and releases gases. These gases form a tail behind the comet.

core—the centermost region of a planet.

crater—an irregular circular or oval hole created by a collision with another object.

density—an object's mass divided by its volume.

diameter—the distance across a round object.

equator—an imaginary circle around the center of Earth, another planet, or the Sun.

friction—a force that resists the motion between two objects or surfaces. If there is motion, energy is converted to heat.

gravity—the force that pulls objects toward the center of a planet and other bodies in space.

magnetic field—the area surrounding a planet in which magnetic force is felt.

magnetosphere—the area of space around a planet that is affected by the planet's magnetic field.

mass—the amount of matter or material in an object.

orbit—the curved path followed by one body going around another body in space.

rotate—to turn or spin around a central point.

solar system—the Sun and all the objects—planets, moons, asteroids, and comets—that orbit it.

space probe—an unmanned spacecraft carrying scientific instruments that orbits the Sun on its way to one or more planets. It may fly past a planet it has been aimed at, orbit the planet, or, in some cases, even land there.

terrain—the physical features of a piece of land.

volume—the total amount of space an object occupies.

To Find Out More

Books

Apfel, Necia. *Voyager to the Planets*. New York: Clarion Books, 1991.

Branley, Franklyn Mansfield. *The Sun And the Solar System*. New York: Twenty-First Century Books, 1996.

Campbell, Peter A. *Launch Day*. Brookfield, CT: Millbrook Press, 1995.

Gardner, Robert. *Space*. New York: Twenty-First Century Books, 1994.

Graham, Ian. *Space Science*. Austin, TX: Raintree Steck-Vaughn, 1993.

Scott, Elaine. *Adventure in Space: The Flight to Fix the Hubble Telescope*. New York: Hyperion Books for Children, 1995.

Vogt, Gregory. *Asteroids, Comets, and Meteors*. Brookfield, CT: Millbrook Press, 1996.

Vogt, Gregory. *Saturn*. Brookfield, CT: Millbrook Press, 1993.

Walker, Jane. *The Solar System*. Brookfield, CT: Millbrook Press, 1995.

Online Sites

Cassini Mission to Saturn
http://www.jpl.nasa.gov/cassini
Learn all about this mission to Saturn.

NASA's Quest Project
http://quest.arc.nasa.gov
A list and description of NASA-sponsored educational programs.

Saturn
http://www.anu.edu.au./physics/nineplanets/saturn.html.
Provides photos of Saturn and information about the planet's atmosphere, interior, moons, and rings.

Saturn's Ring System

http://ringside.arc.nasa.gov/www/saturn/saturn.html.

This site, which is maintained by NASA, has information and images of Saturn's rings and links to other sites. Animations show the movement of the rings and their spokes.

Places to Visit

These museums and science centers are great places to learn more about Saturn and the solar system.

Flandrau Science Center and Planetarium
University of Arizona
Tucson, AZ 85721

Hansen Planetarium
15 South State Street
Salt Lake City, UT 84111

Howell Observatory
1400 W. Mars Hill Rd.
Flagstaff, AZ 86001

Miami Museum of Science and Space Transit Planetarium
3280 South Miami Avenue
Miami, FL 33129

The Newark Museum and Dreyfus Planetarium
49 Washington Street
P.O. Box 540
Newark, NJ 07101-0540

Reuben H. Fleet Space Theater and Science Center
1875 El Prado Way
P.O. Box 33303
San Diego, CA 92163-3303

Schiele Museum of Natural History and Planetarium, Inc.
1500 East Garrison Blvd.
Gastonia, NC 28054

Space Center
Top of New Mexico Highway 2001
P.O. Box 533
Alamogordo, NM 88311-0533

Space Center Houston
1601 NASA Road One
Houston, TX 77058

A Note on Sources

It is important to use as many sources as possible when writing a book about space. I began by reading other books written for young people on my topic. Next, I read standard reference works for general information.

Because scientists learn new information about the planets all the time, I read recent articles in a variety of science magazines and spoke with scientists at NASA's Solar System Exploration Division, the U.S. Space Foundation, and the McDonald Observatory. The Jet Propulsion Laboratory in Pasadena, California, provided me with all the latest facts and figures. I especially appreciated the assistance of Julius L. Benton, Jr., of Associates in Astronomy who checked the accuracy of this manuscript.

—*Elaine Landau*

Index

Numbers in *italics* indicate illustrations.

About the Author

Popular author Elaine Landau has a B.A. degree from New York University and a Master's degree in library and information science from Pratt Institute.

She has written more than 100 non-fiction books for young people. Although Ms. Landau often writes about science, she has particularly enjoyed writing about the planets. She was fascinated to learn about the major strides the space program has made during the last few years.

Elaine Landau lives in Miami, Florida, with her husband and son, Michael. The trio can often be spotted at the Miami Museum of Science and Space Transit Planetarium.